TORNADOES

AND OTHER DRAMATIC WEATHER SYSTEMS

By
Michael Allaby

Consultant
Philip Eden

A Dorling Kindersley Book

Dorling  Kindersley

LONDON, NEW YORK, SYDNEY, DELHI,
PARIS, MUNICH, and JOHANNESBURG

Editors Lucy Hurst and Carey Scott
Designers Ann Cannings and Sheila Collins
Senior Editor Fran Jones
Senior Art Editor Marcus James
Category Publisher Jayne Parsons
Managing Art Editor Jacquie Gulliver
Picture Researcher Jo Haddon
DK Picture Researchers Diane Le Grande and
Rose Horridge
Production Erica Rosen
DTP Designers Matthew Ibbotson and Louise Paddick

First published in Great Britain in 2001 by
Dorling Kindersley Limited
80 The Strand
London WC2R 0RL

2 4 6 8 10 9 7 5 3 1

The CIP Catalogue record for this book is available
from the British Library

ISBN 0-7513-3079-5

Reproduced by Colourscan, Singapore
Printed and bound by L.E.G.O., Italy

See our complete catalogue at
www.dk.com

CONTENTS

INTRODUCTION

Weather is everywhere, sometimes shining on us, other times making us run for cover. It is unpredictable and powerful, so it is good to know what makes it happen. Why does the wind blow? What's going on inside a black storm cloud as lightning flashes, thunder crashes, and rain lashes?

HURRICANE WARNING FLAGS

The sky can be a very violent place. It can produce terrifying tornadoes, with winds fierce enough to demolish houses, throw cars around like toys, and lift whole trains off their tracks. Tornadoes are dangerous storms, but they're usually over quickly, so there's a limit to the damage they do.

Hurricanes are their big brothers – their very big brothers! These are the biggest of all storms. They can be hundreds of kilometres across, with winds near the centre that can blow at more than 240 kmh (150 mph). Sometimes they hurl down so much rain that homes are flooded and villages are buried beneath seas of mud.

Wind and rain are only two of the weapons the weather uses. It can clear the skies and be

A LIFE-SIZED ICE SCULPTURE

hot and sunny – sometimes for too long, so the ground dries, plants die, and people go hungry. Weather can turn the air into a whirling mass of snow so you can't see where you are or what's beneath your feet. It can also produce an ice storm that covers trees and radio masts with a thick coat of ice and freezes roosting birds to their perches.

This book will answer your weather questions. It begins with the most basic question of all. What exactly is weather? It then takes you on a thrilling ride through all kinds of weather, explaining how the noisiest, wettest, coldest, hottest, and windiest types come about. It's not all violence, though. The book also describes some of the weird and beautiful sights that occasionally appear in the sky.

For those of you who want to explore the subject in more detail, there are black Log On "bites" that appear throughout the book. These will direct you to fascinating websites where you can find out even more about tornadoes and other types of extreme weather.

Michael Allaby

WHAT IS WEATHER?

You can't rely on the weather. It changes constantly and sometimes catches us without an umbrella! Driving this change is the Sun. As it brightly beams down, it heats the land and sea, and this makes the air swirl and move across the surface of the planet. This energy causes our daily weather, from sunshine to tornadoes.

Heat of the Sun

The Sun, which generates both life and weather on Earth, is a star – a ferocious ball of fire made of burning gas. Can you imagine what our planet would be like without it? There'd be no sunlight and it would be far too cold for plants or animals to survive. The Sun's rays are a sizzling 5,500°C (9, 900°F), but by the time they reach Earth, the temperature is just right for life to flourish.

S easonal weather

The Sun affects our day-to-day weather, and also our weather over the course of the year. It all depends on the season. Most places have four seasons – spring, summer, autumn, and winter, but countries near the Equator have two seasons – wet and dry – instead.

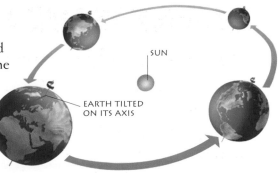

SUN

EARTH TILTED ON ITS AXIS

SEASONS CHANGE BECAUSE EARTH SPINS AROUND THE SUN ON A TILTED AXIS. THIS MEANS ONE HEMISPHERE GETS MORE SUN THAN THE OTHER FOR HALF THE YEAR.

The seasons occur because the amount of sunlight reaching you varies. In summer you get more Sun shining down than you do in winter. This is because, as the Earth orbits around the Sun once a year, its axis is tilted to one side. Therefore first one half – either the northern or southern hemisphere – and then the other is tilted to face the Sun. It's summer – and summer weather – in the hemisphere

that's facing the Sun and winter in the other half. Because of the way seasons work, people in North America will be stuck in snow at the same time as people in Australia have a summer party.

A BURNER KEEPS THE AIR INSIDE A HOT AIR BALLOON WARMER, AND THEREFORE LIGHTER, THAN THE AIR OUTSIDE, SO IT FLOATS.

Hot air

Wherever you are, weather is the way the air around you changes all the time. When the surface of the land and sea are warmed by the Sun, the air above them is also warmed. When air is warmed it rises above cold air. As the warm air rises, cooler air rushes in to take its place.

Gradually this air also becomes warmed and rises, to be replaced by more cold air. Air is continually circulating between the cold, upper regions of the atmosphere and its warm, lower regions. This circular movement of air goes on all the time and causes much of our weather.

Air masses

But there are other types of air movement. Sometimes, vast masses of air move across continents and oceans, and this movement also generates our weather. Think of the air over the middle of a continent – it's fairly dry and hot because there is not much water on the land below. But air over an ocean is different – it's moist and cool because of the huge surface of water underneath. As these air masses move, they slowly change. Air from the continent crosses the ocean and becomes moister, and air from the ocean crosses a continent and becomes drier.

Air masses – as they're called – bring their own kinds of weather to the lands they cross. An air mass that has settled for

LOG ON...
http://kidscience.ics/weatherforkids/index.htm
kidscience.about.com/kids/

same speed so they often collide. Where they meet, cold air pushes beneath warm air, or the warm air rides over the cold air. Either way, the warm air is lifted above the ground. The boundary between the two kinds of air is called a front. It's a cold front if the colder air is behind, and a warm front if there's warmer air behind. Both kinds of fronts make clouds which bring lots of rain – so look out for them on your weather forecast!

Wet air

Clouds form because air contains water vapour – an invisible gas. How much water vapour air contains depends on

AS AIR WARMS UP IT EXPANDS AND RISES INTO THE SKY

several days over the Arctic, for instance, will become very cold, bringing cold weather wherever it moves. An air mass that has moved from the tropics brings warm weather.

Cold fronts, warm fronts

Air masses don't all move at the

where the air mass formed. If it began its life over an ocean, the air will be damper than if it formed over land. Water evaporates (changes from liquid to gas) when it's warm, and condenses (changes back to liquid) when it's cold. You can see this happen in winter, when you get in the car and water from your warm breath condenses onto cold windows.

When water in our atmosphere condenses into droplets, it forms clouds of different shapes and sizes. Cloud droplets merge with one another and grow bigger until they fall to Earth as rain, hail, or snow. You wouldn't think the Sun's heat could make snow fall, but it does – by warming the ground and making water evaporate.

Shallow sky

When it is not snowing or raining, go outside and take a look up. From down here, it seems as though the sky – our name for the Earth's atmosphere – goes on forever. In actual fact, it's not very deep at all compared with the size of the Earth. If the Earth was the size of an orange that had just been washed, the atmosphere is only about as thick as the water on the orange skin.

Earth's atmosphere

The part of the atmosphere that makes weather – and life – possible, is even smaller. The atmosphere is layered, and all our weather happens in the

PLANES FLY ABOVE THE TROPOSPHERE AND THE CLOUDS BECAUSE THEY NEED LESS FUEL IN THE THIN AIR.

troposphere, which is the layer closest to Earth. The troposphere varies in height between 10–16 km (6–10 miles), and contains almost all the atmosphere's water and air. Gravity hugs these weather ingredients close to our planet, which is why there's no weather out in space.

WEIRD WORLD
THERE IS ENOUGH WATER
IN THE TROPOSPHERE
TO FLOOD THE EARTH
TO A DEPTH OF
1 M (3.3 FT).

Fading into space
If you've ever climbed up a mountain you'll know that the air gets colder the higher you climb. It goes on getting cooler all the way up to the top of the troposphere. Then you get to the tropopause, a boundary that rising air can't usually cross. There are several more layers before the atmosphere dwindles out with no definite end – it just slowly fades into the vacuum of space. There's still some air above about 100 km (60 miles), but it

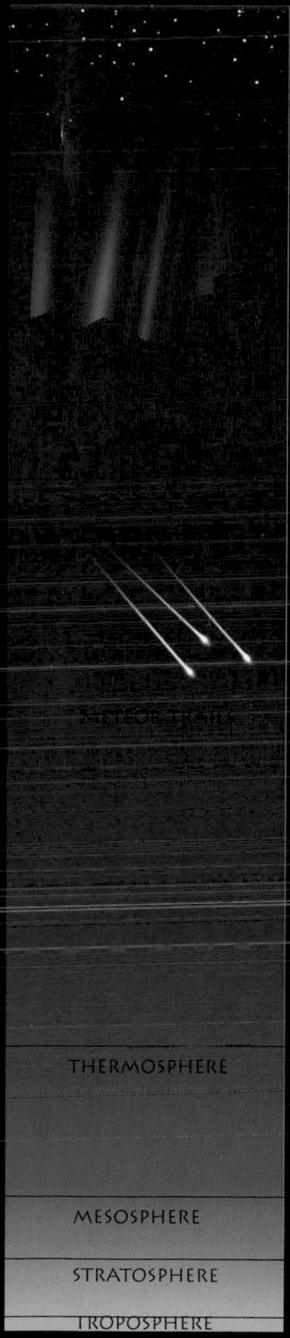

METEOR TRAILS

THERMOSPHERE

MESOSPHERE

STRATOSPHERE

TROPOSPHERE

LAYERS OF THE EARTH'S ATMOSPHERE

contains almost no oxygen so nothing could live there.

Under pressure

Air is very light, but it's not weightless. The weight of the air in the atmosphere pressing down on us is called air pressure. This pressure varies constantly because the weight of the atmosphere presses down more heavily in some places than in others.

AIR PRESSURE IS MEASURED BY A BAROMETER IN UNITS CALLED MILLIBARS

air to breathe if you're doing anything active. That's why mountain climbers carry bottled air and breathe through oxygen masks.

How wind forms

Air moves away from areas of high pressure to areas of low pressure to fill the space. The moving air is what we call wind. The bigger the difference between a high-pressure area and a low one, the faster wind rushes from

WIND BLOWS AROUND AREAS OF HIGH AND LOW PRESSURE

Where air is heavy the pressure is high and where it's not as heavy the pressure is low. These are marked "H" and "L" on weather maps. Low pressure usually means wet, cloudy weather and high pressure indicates a dry, clear day.

The higher you go up the less air there is, because it becomes less squeezed together. If you go above about 3 km (10,000 ft) there's not enough

one to the other – sometimes fast enough to blow off your hat or even the roof of your house!

Currents of wind

Wind blows harder over the oceans because there aren't any obstacles to slow it down. It pushes the water along, as waves, in the direction of the wind, forming ocean currents. Currents are like rivers, only they flow between "banks" made of water rather than land. There are systems of currents in all the oceans. They carry warmth away from the Equator, for example, helping to distribute the Sun's energy more evenly over the surface of Earth.

Windy fun
Wind can be fun. Imagine how hard it would be to fly kites or windsurf without it! A tailwind – one that comes from behind you – makes riding a bike a lot easier too. The trouble is that sooner or later you'll turn a corner and the tailwind will turn into a headwind – one coming straight at you – and then you'll have to pedal harder!

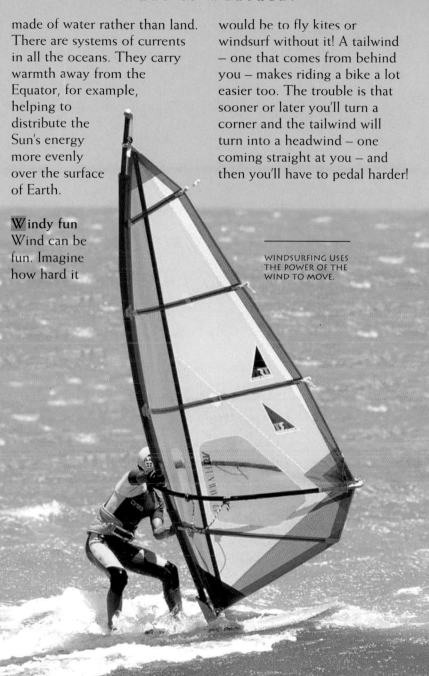

WINDSURFING USES THE POWER OF THE WIND TO MOVE.

CALM SKIES, ANGRY SKIES

Most bad weather involves water. The trouble usually starts when water vapour in the air condenses to form clouds. Fog (low-lying cloud) can cause drivers to have road accidents, but clouds at higher levels are capable of much worse. They can flood huge areas with rain, flatten fields of crops with an onslaught of hail, and make the air explode with lightning flashes.

Cloudspotting

Look out of your window at the sky. Is it cloudy today? Whether the sky looks calm or angry depends on the type of formations are classified by meteorologists into 10 basic types, according to their shape and height. Each of these types belongs to one of three groups

THEY MAY LOOK LUMPY, BUT ALL CLOUDS ARE MADE OF WATER

cloud up there. Some clouds make the whole sky white or grey. Others turn the sky black and bring ferocious storms that flash with lightning and roar with thunder. There are clouds like thin wisps and still others that are small, bright white, and lumpy like cottonwool.

All these different cloud of clouds: stratus (layered), cumulus (lumpy), and cirrus clouds (wispy). Despite their differences, all clouds are formed in the same way.

How clouds are formed

Clouds form when warm air rises and then cools down. When it cools, the water

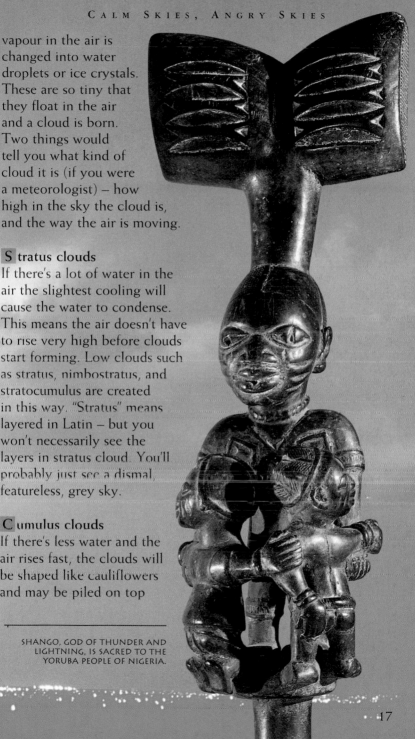

vapour in the air is changed into water droplets or ice crystals. These are so tiny that they float in the air and a cloud is born. Two things would tell you what kind of cloud it is (if you were a meteorologist) – how high in the sky the cloud is, and the way the air is moving.

Stratus clouds

If there's a lot of water in the air the slightest cooling will cause the water to condense. This means the air doesn't have to rise very high before clouds start forming. Low clouds such as stratus, nimbostratus, and stratocumulus are created in this way. "Stratus" means layered in Latin – but you won't necessarily see the layers in stratus cloud. You'll probably just see a dismal, featureless, grey sky.

Cumulus clouds

If there's less water and the air rises fast, the clouds will be shaped like cauliflowers and may be piled on top

SHANGO, GOD OF THUNDER AND LIGHTNING, IS SACRED TO THE YORUBA PEOPLE OF NIGERIA.

of each other. The small, white, lumpy clouds that drift across summer skies are called fair-weather cumulus. But not all cumulus clouds mean sunny and calm weather. They can grow bigger and bigger until they turn into "cumulonimbus". They're the nasty ones that bring rain, hail, snow – often thunderstorms and sometimes even tornadoes.

Cirrus clouds

Very dry air has to rise even higher before it's cold enough for the water vapour to condense. When it does, it is so cold that the vapour condenses as tiny ice crystals rather than water droplets. These high clouds have

A CUMULONIMBUS
STORM CLOUD
ABOUT TO UNLOOSE
ITS FEROCIOUS
ENERGY ONTO
THE EARTH.

"cirrus" or "cirro" in their names. Cirrus, cirrostratus, and cirrocumulus are all high-level clouds and look a long way up.

LENTICULAR CLOUDS CAN HOVER IN THE SAME SPOT FOR HOURS, RESEMBLING "FLYING SAUCERS" OR UFOS.

Weird clouds
As you know, weather is often unpredictable, so it is not surprising that warm air doesn't always go straight up. On land, it's forced to rise when it crosses a mountain, but it may sink again on the other side. This can set the flow of air moving up and down in waves, like the waves on water. When this happens, cloud sometimes forms near the crest of each wave. These lenticular (lens-shaped) clouds are white, smooth, shaped like saucers, and can look like UFOs.

Forming fog
Water vapour can also condense at ground level to form fog.

CUMULUS CLOUDS CAN BRING SUN OR STORMS

19

That is, stratus cloud that lies on the ground. Fog often forms at night, when the ground grows cold and chills the lowest layer of air. Warm, moist air drifting over cold ground or water, creates perfect fog conditions – so that's why it often forms over seas and lakes.

far you can see. Experts reckon that if you can still see objects that are about 1 km (0.6 mile) away then you are in mist. If you can't see that far then it must be fog. Neither should be confused with smog, which is caused by pollution, and can be so thick that visibility can drop to just 15 m (50 ft) or less.

Mist, fog, and smog

Sometimes people talk about mist rather than fog. But mist is just thin fog. Next time you find yourself in a fog, check how

Rainclouds

It may not look wet, but if you've walked through fog you'll know how damp it feels. Fog droplets don't move about enough to grow into rain, but cloud droplets do. They bump, collide, and merge until they're so heavy they fall from the cloud. Small drops fall as drizzle, bigger drops are born as raindrops.

If the air temperature inside the cloud is below freezing, ice crystals form instead of raindrops. These may link together to make snowflakes. But, if on their way towards the ground, the temperature is above freezing, the snowflakes will melt and fall as rain. Most of the rain that falls over Europe and North America is melted snow, even in summer.

When rain freezes

It can be really violent inside big storm clouds. You wouldn't want to get caught between warm air pushing up and ice and snow falling downwards in bitterly cold air. Ice and snow are melted by rising warm air

THE GOLDEN GATE BRIDGE IN SAN FRANCISCO, USA, DRAPED WITH FOG.

WEIRD WORLD
A CANADIAN AIRFIELD WAS FORCED TO CLOSE BECAUSE OF VERY LOW-LYING FOG – THE SKY WAS COMPLETELY CLEAR BUT PILOTS COULDN'T SEE THE RUNWAYS!

PEOPLE IN CHINA SHELTER FROM THE RAIN AS THEY CYCLE TO WORK AND SCHOOL.

Farmers' nightmare Hurtling hailstones can cause damage to crops in just minutes, by pelting vegetation and fruit at great force. Farmers have attempted to save their crops from hail for centuries, but with little success. In Europe, in about 1900, farmers fired specially made cannons into

and become raindrops at the bottom of the cloud. This warm air also sweeps the drops back to the top of the cloud and they freeze again. As an ice pellet falls through the cloud, water droplets freeze onto it. The stone is picked up by an updraught, then dropped again, and each time it falls it grows a new layer of ice. Eventually they're so big they fall to Earth as hailstones.

Most hailstones are less than the size of a golf ball, but one that fell in Bangladesh in 1986 was reported to have weighed an astonishing 1 kg (2.2 lb).

GIANT HAIL CAUSES HAVOC ON THE ROADS IN SHAMROCK, TEXAS, USA.

the sky – hoping that water would condense onto the smoke particles, and become rain instead of hail. In the 1960s, the Russians revived the idea, this time using artillery shells and rockets. But hail has proved unstoppable! Today, hailstorms are just as frequent and damaging.

Thunder and lightning

Storms that throw down huge hailstones often also flash with lightning. A lightning stroke is an electric spark, but it's no ordinary spark. It carries an electric current of between 10,000 and 40,000 amps. If it hits a tree, a lightning stroke can instantly boil all the water inside it making the tree explode like a bomb. Toothpick anyone?

Exploding air

Did you know that lightning causes thunder? As it flashes, lightning heats the air around it by up to 33,000°C (59,400°F) in less than a second. This makes the air explode outwards and thunder is the sound of that explosion.

Creating a thunderstorm

To produce a thunderstorm, cumulonimbus clouds must be

LIGHTNING'S HEAT CAN FUSE SANDY SOIL INTO THE SHAPE OF THE ELECTRICITY'S PATH, CREATING A FORMATION CALLED A FULGURITE.

tall enough for ice crystals to form near the top. Then, rising ice-crystals brush past falling water droplets causing parts of the cloud to become electrically charged. These charges build up to millions of volts and suddenly spark. When they

ever knowing what hit you. Only 50–60 per cent of people struck by lightning survive the experience. An American park ranger was struck by lightning no fewer than seven times! Eventually, he died peacefully in his sleep.

Lightning advice

If you happen to see those dark cumulonimbus clouds gathering, here are a few tips to help you dodge disaster. If you're outside, stay away from anything tall or wet – trees and water are bad news because they both act as electricity conductors. Your best bet is to find somewhere low down, such as a dry ditch, and lie in it.

If you're inside, close the doors and windows. Don't phone your friends or watch

AIR HEATED BY LIGHTNING IS FIVE TIMES HOTTER THAN THE SUN

spark, a bolt of lightning flashes. It may flash between different parts of the same cloud, between two separate clouds, or between a cloud and the ground.

If you're struck by lightning, you might be killed without

television. Outdoor phone lines and TV aerials can act as conductors. Weather can be very dangerous as well as unpredictable!

LIGHTNING STRIKES THE EIFFEL TOWER IN PARIS, FRANCE.

TORNADOES

A tornado, or twister, is the most violent concentration of energy the atmosphere can produce. It's a column of spinning air, and near its centre the wind can be blowing at more than 400 kmh (250 mph). Tornadoes occur in many parts of the world and can be devastating. A tornado can suck up a wooden house and spit it out in splinters. It can lift an entire train from the tracks, and turn a truck into a mess of twisted steel.

A TORNADO, SURROUNDED BY AN EERIE CALM, STRIKES A FARMHOUSE IN KANSAS, USA.

LOG ON...
www.nws.noaa.gov/
om/tornado.htm

Birth of a tornado

So how does this giant suction machine start out? Tornadoes form inside huge storm clouds known as supercells. These are fuelled by warm air, which is drawn in at the base of the cloud and rises upwards in powerful air currents. In the same way that water disappearing down a plughole starts rotating, so these warm updraughts start spinning. If the spin becomes sufficiently intense, the rotating air extends below the cloud base as a funnel. Once this funnel touches the ground it becomes a tornado – and it's time to take cover!

Outbreaks

When several tornadoes happen at once you have a tornado outbreak. These are often caused by squall lines. These are lines of storm

WEIRD WORLD
IN OKLAHOMA, A SMALL HERD OF CATTLE WERE SUCKED UP BY A TORNADO AND CARRIED ACROSS THE COUNTRYSIDE, BEFORE BEING SET DOWN UNHARMED.

- ○ 3–4 A YEAR
- ○ 2–3 A YEAR
- ● 1–2 A YEAR
- ● LESS THAN ONE A YEAR

THE MAP SHOWS THE NUMBER OF
TORNADOES PER 50-MILE (130-KM) SQUARE
THAT HIT TORNADO ALLEY.

cloud, up to 1,000 km
(600 miles) long. Each storm
lasts for only an hour or two,
but as it dies down it triggers
another. Squall lines can
happen almost anywhere, but
they are most frequent and
most violent over the states in
the middle of the USA. This is
where cold air from the Arctic
meets very warm, moist air
from the Gulf of Mexico and
hot, dry air from the deserts of
Arizona and New Mexico.

The area suffers from so
many twisters – hundreds each
year – that it has become
known as Tornado Alley. But,
although tornadoes are best
known for terrorizing America's
Great Plains, they occur in

28

many parts of the world. Even the UK, well-known for its moderate climate, gets about 60 tornadoes a year.

Tornado terror

Being caught in a tornado can be terrifying. Some lucky people get a warning and can move to a safe place. For example, in 1974 a group of high-school children in Ohio, USA, took cover from a tornado in a ground-floor corridor of their school. They huddled together while the tornado ripped through the building. When the danger had passed, the students emerged to a strange sight. They found a school bus on the stage where, only minutes earlier, they had been rehearsing their school play. The bus had been picked up from the street and dropped

WRECKED HOMES AND UPROOTED TREES IN GEORGIA, USA, AFTER A TORNADO IN 1994.

through the roof by the tornado! Those kids were lucky. The tornado took just 20 minutes to wreck nearly 3,000 buildings and kill 34 people in their town.

Pressure drop

Tornadoes are extremely destructive because of the sudden drop in air pressure they bring. At the centre of a tornado is a low-pressure vortex, a whirling mass of motion, usually about 2 km (1 mile) wide. This acts like a giant vacuum cleaner, capable of sucking up animals, people,

Flying vehicles

During a tornado, vehicles (like the school bus), furniture, planks of wood, and other debris become deadly weapons as they are hurled through the air at tremendous speed. And, because objects picked up by tornadoes may be kept in the air until the winds die down,

SMALL TORNADOES SOMETIMES FORM AT THE EDGES OF BIG ONES

entire buildings – and spitting them out again. It sweeps over the ground, reducing all in its path to rubble. A tornado can demolish a row of houses and mix up the furniture so completely that you might find your stuff down the road in a friend's house! Yet tornadoes can seem to be selective in their destruction – it is not unusual for one side of a street to be demolished while the other remains completely untouched.

they can travel a long way. After a tornado hit a town in Nebraska, USA, a baby grand piano was found in a field, some 365 m (400 yd) from its home.

Take cover

If you see a really black storm cloud with a funnel of cloud attached to its base, the best thing to do is take cover – but

THIS TORNADO HAS JUST HIT THE GROUND, AND ITS BASE IS BLACK WITH DUST AND DEBRIS,

not inside a caravan or mobile home, because that won't stay put in the wind. Stay away from windows – debris may come crashing through them, shooting splinters of glass in all directions. If possible, lie down under a heavy table or a mattress. If you can't do that, squat on your heels. Don't try to run away from a tornado. There's no way to

predict the direction it will move and it can whisk across the ground at up to 95 kmh (60 mph).

Shelter from the storm

Some people who live in Tornado Alley, or other tornado-prone areas, have specially built storm shelters in their back gardens. These are underground rooms with heavy doors that can be fastened tightly. When the National Weather Service issues a "tornado watch" warning, people get inside and stay there until the danger has passed.

A SCENE FROM THE 1998 FILM TWISTER, SHOWS STORM CHASERS ON THE TRAIL OF A TORNADO.

S torm chasers

When a tornado appears over the horizon most sensible folk head for cover. But some don't. They're the scientists – sometimes called storm chasers – who study tornadoes.

Studying tornadoes is very tricky. In the first place they're not easy to find because they come and go very quickly. Then, if you do see one and get close enough to examine it, it's more than likely to wreck your instruments, your car, and you. But the scientists know what they're doing.

Storm chasers from the Severe Storms Laboratory in Oklahoma built a really strong package of instruments sealed inside a metal cylinder in a

A BUILT-IN SCREEN AT THIS US PETROL PUMP DISPLAYS TORNADO MOVEMENTS TO CUSTOMERS.

ON OPEN LAND, TORNADOES LEAVE SCARS LIKE A GIANT'S FOOTPRINT

super-strong iron frame. It could measure and record wind speed, pressure, temperature, and electrical disturbances. They called it the Totable Tornado Observatory, or TOTO for short after the dog in the film *The Wizard of Oz*, which, as you probably know, featured a tornado. They would leave TOTO in the path of a

tornado and let it take the strain while they kept clear.

Nowadays storm chasers use Doppler radar. This is a radar device that allows scientists to actually watch a developing vortex inside a storm cloud.

Tornadoes are just one type of whirlwind. There are others that are created in the same way, but behave differently.

33

WATERSPOUTS AND DUST DEVILS

When tornadoes move over lakes or the sea they become waterspouts. These look like white, twisting columns of water reaching high into the sky. They can wreck boats and suck up fish or frogs and drop them miles away. Out in the desert there's a different kind of danger. It's a tower of swirling dust and sand called a dust devil.

Wet whirlwind

Although they look like spouts of water being sucked up, waterspouts are actually mostly made of water vapour. We can see a spout because water vapour inside the low pressure vortex condenses to form cloud. The water you may see splashing at the base is actually created when a waterspout lashes the surface of the lake or sea into a cloud of spray called a spray ring. This doesn't sound as if it would cause much damage, but a spray ring can literally be full of tonnes of water. No joke if it drops on your boat!

Danger!

Waterspouts have even drowned people who watched from shore, thinking they were safe. A waterspout off the coast of Spain killed six people by dumping tonnes of water onto a pier, sweeping the people into the sea.

Forming on water

Not all waterspouts start out as tornadoes. Some actually form over water. No one really knows what makes this kind form, because it is very hard to be in the right place to study them! These waterspouts are not as ferocious as tornadoes and are usually less than 100 m (300 ft)

WATERSPOUT AND LIGHTNING DURING A FLORIDA THUNDERSTORM, IN THE USA

IS THIS A GLIMPSE OF SCOTLAND'S
LOCH NESS MONSTER? IT'S MORE
LIKELY TO BE A WATER DEVIL.

devil – appears over lakes. It happens when cool winds flow off hills and meet over warm water. This makes the air curve into a vortex and move across the water.

It's likely that some of the sightings of the Loch Ness monster in Scotland have actually been water devils. From a distance, a small column of cloud darting about over the surface of a lake, with a spray ring bulging around its base, could easily be mistaken for a strange creature by an over-eager monster-spotter!

in diameter at the base and generate winds of no more than 80 kmh (50 mph). You're most

RARE WATER DEVILS CAN ONLY FORM OVER LAKES

likely to see waterspouts – those that form on water – in a bay of warm water in autumn.

Sometimes waterspouts – of both kinds – sweep up fish and frogs in their spray rings, and then drop them miles away once the wind has dropped. So if you ever find yourself in a shower of sticklebacks, you'll know a waterspout's nearby!

Water devil

A much rarer kind of small waterspout – called a water

Dust devils

Dust devils are more familiar than water devils and can be truly frightening. They usually appear in the afternoon, especially in desert regions where areas of the ground get really hot. Air over the hot ground rises fast because it's heated quickly, and the surrounding, cooler air is drawn in at ground level. Sand is sucked in with the cool air and is carried up with it to create a whirlwind of hot sand.

Dust everywhere! Then, suddenly without warning and beneath a clear blue sky, the devil leaps from the ground, a twisting tower of screaming wind, often 30 m (100 ft) high – although they can be up to 2 km (1.2 miles) tall. It lasts for only a few minutes, but watch out! As it dies down another one often rises nearby, and then another.

Although they are less destructive than tornadoes, dust devils are still capable of demolishing flimsy buildings – and of throwing a lot of sand in your eyes!

WEIRD WORLD

DUST DEVILS OCCUR ON MARS. THE PLANET IS COVERED BY A LAYER OF DUST AND HAS FIERCE WINDS THAT BLOW ACROSS THE SURFACE, SOMETIMES CREATING DUST DEVILS.

HURRICANES

From space it's beautiful. A disc of pure white cloud with a hole in the middle. But for those caught in its grip, it is a nightmare of screaming wind, flying debris, lashing rain, and huge seas. We're talking about a hurricane. At least, in the Atlantic it's a hurricane – in the northwest Pacific it's called a typhoon, and in the Indian Ocean it's a cyclone. Whatever you call it, it is the biggest and most destructive storm on Earth.

Birth of a hurricane

How does all this havoc begin? Imagine a thunderstorm brewing over the tropics, or on land, for example, in north Africa. Next, imagine It takes most of the summer for the sea to warm up this much, which is why the Atlantic hurricane season generally lasts from late summer until late autumn.

THE NAME TYPHOON IS THE CHINESE WORD FOR "BIG WIND"

the storm being carried westwards, and away from the Equator, by strong winds over a vast ocean, such as the Atlantic. Here, it may encounter the special conditions a hurricane needs to build up to its mighty and monstrous conclusion.

Most importantly, the temperature of the sea surface must be at least 27°C (80°F).

Driving the storm

As the sea gets warmer and warmer, huge amounts of sea water evaporate. This vapour then rises and condenses into storm clouds that tower to a height of about 17 km (56,000 ft). Air is sucked in from below the clouds to join the rising current. As air approaches the clouds, it begins to turn anti-clockwise in the northern hemisphere and clockwise in the southern hemisphere.

Spinning winds

The storm spins because of the Coriolis effect – when wind is moved in a curve by the Earth rotating below. There is no Coriolis effect at the Equator, which is why hurricanes never form close to it. When the winds spinning around the centre of the storm reach speeds of more than 120 kmh (75 mph) the storm is officially called a hurricane. The winds that are generated are so powerful they could literally sweep you off your feet.

Faster and faster

Air accelerates as it spirals in towards the centre of the storm, just like it spirals into the centre of a tornado. The further it travels to get there, the faster it goes, like a bike speeding down a spiral ramp without brakes. So, the bigger the storm – and on average it can be

500–800 km (310–500 miles) across – the stronger its winds will be.

The eye of the storm

Bizarrely, at the centre of this frightening and swirling mass of cloud the sky is clear, and the air is warm and still. This area of calm is called the eye,

WHEN A HURRICANE HAS BEEN FORECAST, THESE WARNING FLAGS ARE RAISED TO LET PEOPLE KNOW.

and it's usually 10–60 km (6.2–37 miles) across. That's why there's always an ominous lull during a hurricane that you might mistake for the end of the storm – but it's actually only the halfway point as the eye passes overhead. Surrounding the eye there's a circle of the hurricane's biggest storm clouds. That's where you find the heaviest rain and the fiercest winds.

Rain drain

These immense, violent clouds dump huge amounts of rain. In 1998 Hurricane Mitch, which killed at least 11,000 people in Central America and the Caribbean, dropped an

Sea surges

But it's not just rain water that causes problems. Hurricanes also cause a small sea level rise, because the air pressure is much lower at the eye of the storm, so the water expands. The hurricane's winds also drive ocean waves towards the shore and the stronger the wind, the bigger and more ferocious the waves.

The combination of these huge waves and a high tide creates a storm surge. If waves reach the shore when there's a higher than normal tide, during a spring tide for example, the result is a massive storm surge. Huge walls of water rush inland, sweeping away

THE MOST POWERFUL WINDS ARE CLOSE TO THE EYE OF THE STORM

estimated total of 1,900 mm (75 in) of rain over the 11 days that it raged. Almost 635 mm (25 in) fell in Honduras within 6 hours. That's more than London, UK, receives in a whole year. It is hardly surprising, then, that hurricanes cause bad floods and that the build up of water causes the most damage.

buildings, trees, animals, and people.

Hurricane Mitch came ashore with waves up to 13 m (44 ft) high – that is as high as a three-storey house. Imagine how scary it would be to see those waves rolling in from the sea! These terrifying storm surges account for most of the deaths caused by hurricanes.

Classifying winds

Every hurricane in the Atlantic is given a name by the National Hurricane Center in Florida, USA. Sometimes, there are several at the same time, so naming hurricanes makes it easy to tell them apart. Each name moves on to start with the next letter of the alphabet, and boys' and girls' names alternate.

The names are drawn from a list that is compiled for the six years ahead. In the seventh year the names revert to the first list.

If there's been a really devastating hurricane, its name may

SATELLITE PHOTO OF HURRICANE ELENA, CLEARLY SHOWING THE EYE OF THE STORM.

mangrove forests. Animals have to try and survive, just like us. Migratory birds can be blown thousands of kilometres off their usual routes, ending up dazed and confused in strange lands. Or worse: in 1989 Hurricane Hugo almost wiped out the whole population of an endangered species of woodpecker in South Carolina, USA.

be withdrawn from the list.

Hurricane Andrew, in 1993, was the most expensive in American history. Its destruction in Florida and Louisiana cost an estimated US$25 billion to repair. For this reason, its name won't be used again.

Hurricanes are much stronger than the scale used for normal winds, so, in 1955, the US Weather Bureau introduced a new 5-point scale. A hurricane rating of just 1 can damage trees and flimsy buildings, while a hurricane rating 5 will cause extensive flooding and major damage to all buildings less than 4.5 m (15 ft) above sea level.

Plants and animals

It's not just people and property that are damaged by hurricanes. Huge storm waves can severely damage coastal habitats such as coral reefs and

Forecasting hurricanes

Hurricanes are killers. Fortunately, meteorologists can usually see them coming, and can try to predict the path the hurricane will follow. Weather satellites send a constant stream of measurements and pictures to receiving stations on the ground. In the case of Atlantic storms, this information is collected at the National Hurricane Center in Florida. Aircraft called hurricane trackers fly through the storm, radioing details back to the Hurricane

RESIDENTS OF FLORIDA KEYS, USA, BATTLE AGAINST 1998'S HURRICANE GEORGES.

Center. When the hurricane comes within range of a weather radar, the size of the storm clouds, the amount of rain they're producing, and the direction and speed of winds around the eye are all revealed.

Emergency services use this information to issue warnings to communities likely to be affected. If the hurricane is a severe one, people who live in its path may be evacuated. But the forecasters don't always get it right. Hurricanes can change direction or strike unexpectedly, and they are still responsible for thousands of deaths every year.

LOG ON...
www.hurricanehunters.com

Energy release

As a hurricane reaches land, it quickly subsides because it has lost contact with the warm water that fuels it. Once it has released its energy onto the the coast, it dies out. But some hurricanes remain over the sea where they last much longer. They're weakening all the time they move away from warm, tropical waters, but some cross the Atlantic and still have enough strength to cause havoc in Europe.

Hurricane in Europe

In October 1987 the remains of Hurricane Floyd took the weather forecasters by surprise and swept along the south coast of England. Although barely a

HURRICANE ANDREW, IN 1992, FLIPPED A VAN ON TOP OF A CAR – LUCKILY BOTH VEHICLES WERE EMPTY.

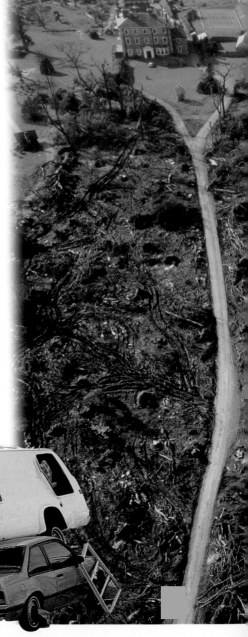

category-1 hurricane, Floyd was powerful enough to kill 19 people and uproot 19 million trees, including many rare specimens in the Royal Botanic Gardens at Kew, London.

B e prepared

If you live in an area where hurricanes happen, be prepared for them.

• Find out how far above sea level your home is and how far it is from the coast. This will give you an idea of the risk from storm surges.

• Work out the fastest route to high ground in case you're told to evacucate.

• If a hurricane strikes, listen to bulletins on the radio or television and always obey their instructions.

• If there is a room in your house or school without any outside walls, stay in it while the hurricane passes.

• When the wind starts, lie on the floor, if possible beneath a strong table.

• Keep away from the windows.

• Don't go outdoors until you're told it's safe.

UPROOTED TREES IN THE SOUTH OF ENGLAND AFTER HURRICANE FLOYD SWEPT ALONG THE SOUTH COAST IN 1987.

BELOW FREEZING

S now changes the world into a wonderland as it falls in big, floating flakes. It can look lovely and also means it's time for winter sports. But if you live somewhere with severe winters, you'll know that snow can be dangerous too, especially if roads are blocked and someone needs to get to hospital quickly. Worst of all, avalanches can hurl tonnes of snow down mountainsides, taking rocks, trees – and skiers – with them!

What is snow?

Snow forms when tiny ice crystals in clouds stick together to make snowflakes. When these grow large enough, they fall out of clouds as snow, and swirl towards the ground. Snowflakes land everywhere – on cars, trees and even your eyelashes! When you walk on snow, it "crunches" under your feet because air is trapped between flakes. In fact, snow is mostly air, which makes it very bulky and heavy.

Why does it snow?

Outside the tropics, most rain is snow that has melted on its way to the ground. But, if the temperature between the clouds and the ground is close to zero degrees C (32°F), it will fall as snow. If the temperature of the ground is freezing, the snow will settle – that means you'll be able to make a snowman. The heaviest snowfalls occur when the air temperature is around freezing. But, strangely, if it dips too far below freezing it may be too cold to snow. This is because very cold air

IF YOU LOOKED UNDER A MICROSCOPE, YOU'D SEE THAT NO TWO SNOWFLAKES ARE THE SAME – JUST LIKE FINGERPRINTS.

Mount Whitney, which once received an incredible 10 m (33 ft) of snow in one month.

B lizzard

Snow doesn't always fall in gentle flakes. If the wind is fierce, a blizzard will drive snow horizontally. Sometimes, the wind will actually whip

IT HARDLY EVER SNOWS AT THE POLES BECAUSE IT'S TOO COLD

may not hold enough moisture to make snow.

Canada and the US get more snow than most parts of the world. The snowiest place in North America is Tamarack on the slopes of California's

light, powdery snow off the ground and make a blizzard. Severe blizzards hit North America every winter, but they have been known to happen as close to the Equator as Lebanon and southern Turkey.

BLIZZARD CONDITIONS NEAR CAEN IN FRANCE FORCED THESE DRIVERS TO STOP THEIR CARS. ONE PERSON FROZE TO DEATH DURING THIS SNOWSTORM.

A whiteout – as it's called – is very dangerous. Blinding clouds of snow can reduce visibility to 10 m (33 ft), causing drivers to veer off roads and walkers to lose their sense of direction.

The wind can blow huge drifts of snow against walls, hedges, and other obstacles, completely burying cars, trains, and people under snowdrifts.

A SNOWBOARDER
FLIES THROUGH THE AIR.

Wind chill
Winds, like those that create a blizzard, can make cold weather feel even colder. This is because wind carries heat away from your body quickly, making the air feel much colder than it really is. You've probably heard weather forecasters talking about the "wind chill factor". In a strong wind, a temperature of –7°C (19.4°F) can have a wind chill factor of –29°C (–20.2°F). Brrrrrrrr!

Whiteout
A severe blizzard can have winds of more than 72 kmh (45 mph) and a wind chill temperature of about –39°C (–38.2°F). It can also make everything white, including the air, the sky, and the ground.

Avalanche
On mountainsides deep snow brings another danger – the avalanche. A huge slide of snow may sound like fun, but anyone caught in the path of an avalanche – which can be 800 m (half a mile) wide, and travel at speeds of 160 kmh (100 mph) – has just a 5 per cent chance of survival.

Most avalanches occur where thick snow lies on medium slopes. If the slope is too shallow, the snow won't move.

AN AVALANCHE IS ABOUT TO HIT THE SKI RESORT OF TELLURIDE IN SOUTHWEST COLORADO, USA.

If it's too steep, the snow slides off before it gets deep enough to cause any harm.

Then something happens to destabilize the snow. It may be a further snowfall that increases the weight of snow, or a slight thaw that loosens it. After that, the slightest shock can set the snow sliding. The snap as a tree branch breaks, or the whoosh of a passing skier can be enough to set off an avalanche.

First the snow slides downhill, but soon it starts tumbling, growing into a terrifying, roaring wall of snow that moves faster than a speeding car. A big avalanche can create a hurricane-force wind ahead of the snow. The wind is enough to uproot

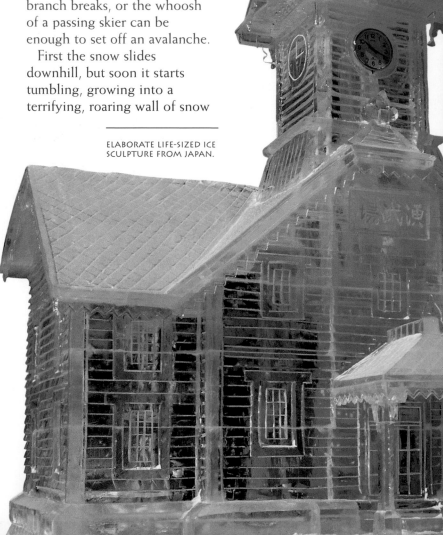

ELABORATE LIFE-SIZED ICE SCULPTURE FROM JAPAN.

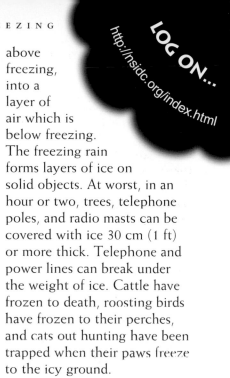

LOG ON...
http://nsidc.org/index.html

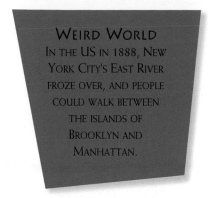

> ## WEIRD WORLD
> IN THE US IN 1888, NEW YORK CITY'S EAST RIVER FROZE OVER, AND PEOPLE COULD WALK BETWEEN THE ISLANDS OF BROOKLYN AND MANHATTAN.

trees and tear roofs off houses, and if you've survived that, the avalanche is right behind – millions of tonnes of snow, and the trees and rocks it sweeps up as it goes.

Ice storm

Sometimes rain can turn to ice. This happens when heavy rain falls from a layer of air which is above freezing, into a layer of air which is below freezing. The freezing rain forms layers of ice on solid objects. At worst, in an hour or two, trees, telephone poles, and radio masts can be covered with ice 30 cm (1 ft) or more thick. Telephone and power lines can break under the weight of ice. Cattle have frozen to death, roosting birds have frozen to their perches, and cats out hunting have been trapped when their paws freeze to the icy ground.

That's an ice storm. It usually happens just before warm weather comes. If you're out walking or riding a bike during an ice storm you'll also grow a coat of ice. It won't be as thick as the ones on the trees, though, because your movement will keep breaking the ice and making it fall.

Ice art

Snow and ice can be fun too. It would be very hard to skate on lakes and ponds without ice! If it's really cold, artists can use ice to create amazing sculptures. In northern Norway they even build entire hotels or palaces from ice. You can stay

THIS COAT IS WORN BY THE NGANASAN PEOPLE, WHO LIVE IN SIBERIA.

made from animal skins, usually decorated in bright colours. There's a good reason for that – bright colours make you visible from a long way off, so if you do get caught in a whiteout you've got a chance of being rescued.

Animal survival

If we go somewhere cold and don't keep wrapped up warm, we lose body heat from blood vessels in the our skin, especially from our ears, fingers, and toes. Animals have to rely on their natural features to keep warm. Emperor penguins huddle together for warmth, and have smaller beaks and flippers than any other penguins, so there is a smaller area losing heat.

there and sleep on an ice bed, sit on ice chairs, eat from ice tables, and enjoy iced drinks. But, like snowmen, ice palaces don't last long. When spring comes they melt and disappear.

Warm and safe

Keeping warm is a major preoccupation for humans and animals living in cold climates. The trick is to trap warm air by wearing lots of layers of clothes. Traditionally, people wore garments

Near the North Pole, the arctic fox and polar bear have very small ears for the same reason. Polar bears are also insulated by their fur. Each hair is hollow and traps body heat like a little "greenhouse".

climate and weather. They drill through the ice and remove a column of ice, called a core. Thin lines in the core mark each year's snowfall. From this, scientists can see what the weather was like in the distant

WATER CAN REMAIN LOCKED UP AS ICE FOR MILLIONS OF YEARS

Weather study

There are no native people living on Antarctica – just people who go to work there as scientists at research stations. Some of them are investigating

past. They've studied ice that is 420,000 years old, and traced detailed changes in climate for the last 100,000 years. Studies like this provide scientists with a more complete picture of the Earth's weather patterns.

EMPEROR PENGUIN CHICKS HUDDLE TOGETHER FOR WARMTH.

TOO MUCH RAIN

NOAH AND THE ANIMALS
ON THE ARK SURVIVED
THE BIBLICAL FLOOD.

Although we need rain, too much is a problem. Rivers overflow into fields, towns, and homes. Roads and bridges are washed away, crops are destroyed, and animals drown. When the floodwater recedes, it leaves a thick, foul-smelling layer of mud behind. Floods cause more damage and kill more people than all other weather disasters combined.

Floods from extreme weather

Severe floods are often a result of other terrible weather events. As you've already

Monsoon floods

Another cause of destruction is monsoon flooding. Most of Southeast Asia is affected by

MONSOON AREAS HAVE WET AND DRY SEASONS, NOT HOT AND COLD

discovered, tornadoes are produced by huge storms that release torrential rain. Hurricanes don't just produce terrifying winds, they also dump huge amounts of rain.

In some hurricanes, much of the damage and deaths result from rain. In 1998, when Hurricane Mitch hit Honduras in Central America, entire villages were washed away, along with most of the country's roads and bridges.

the monsoon winds, which bring heavy rainfall every year between May and October. Monsoon comes from the Arabic word meaning "season".

Monsoons are caused by differences in air pressure over land and sea. Winter is a dry season, but summer is very different. Air pressure over land drops and the winds change

DURING THE MONSOON IN GOA, INDIA,
RIVERS RAGE AND BECOME TREACHEROUS

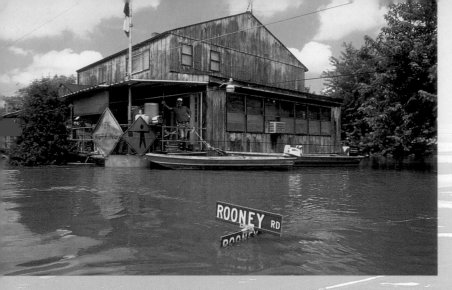

direction, bringing very moist air from the sea. As it crosses the land and is forced to rise, the water vapour condenses into huge clouds and then, for the first time in months, the rain starts to fall.

World-wide destruction

If it rains more than usual during the monsoon, huge areas become flooded in a short time. In 1999 in Bangladesh, roughly one-tenth of the country was covered with water that destroyed crops and drove about 400,000 people from their homes. The people of Bangladesh weren't alone. While they were scrambling to safety, people living along the valley of the Chang Jiang (Yangtze River) in southeastern China were doing the same, and so were the inhabitants of about 2,000 villages in the state of Bihar, India. Flooding can happen anywhere, but is most common in those countries affected by the monsoon.

Water everywhere

The biggest, most spread-out floods usually happen on flat, low-lying land where a big river, such as the Mississippi in the USA, meanders slowly towards the sea. This flat region is called a floodplain. This is because when the amount of water in the river increases, it overflows and floods the plains on either side.

People who live in these areas want to prevent the river flooding, to protect the houses and roads they've built. In some places this has been done by artificially raising the river banks. This protects the floodplain, but it leaves the water with nowhere to go. So instead of covering the floodplain when there's been heavy rain, the water backs up and floods further upstream. The weight of the water then breaks down the raised banks, and floods consume the floodplain after all.

The only way to prevent the destruction of property by this type of flood is to remove the houses and roads and restore the original floodplain, so there's a place where excess water can collect harmlessly.

Climate change

Many scientists believe that flooding can also be a result of climate change. However, this is a much-debated subject and one on which experts cannot agree. There has been no increase in the number or severity of storms over the past 50 years, or in the frequency or ferocity of hurricanes. This indicates that climate change doesn't necessarily mean worse storms or floods.

Violent storms happen when very warm and very cold air collide. If the climate grows warmer in the tropics, or colder in the middle latitudes – where Europe and North America

are – there might be more of these collisions and the weather might grow stormier. Many scientists believe the climate of the world is growing warmer, but that the warming is happening mostly in middle latitudes and near the Poles. This reduces the difference in temperature between the warm tropical and cold polar air, so you should expect fewer storms.

If tropical seas grow warmer, hurricanes could be bigger, more violent, and perhaps more frequent, but some scientists have calculated that they would become weaker and less frequent. There has been an increase in rainfall in northern Europe and northern North America, but it is not certain why. In fact, no one knows what will happen in years to come.

> ### WEIRD WORLD
> IN 1926, A FLOOD ALONG THE MISSISSIPPI RIVER IN THE USA, TURNED THE RIVER INTO AN INLAND SEA COVERING 65,000 SQUARE KM (25,000 SQUARE MILES). IN SOME PLACES IT REACHED A DEPTH OF 5.4 M (18 FT).

CARS ARE BURIED BY A RAIN-INDUCED MUDSLIDE IN CALIFORNIA, USA.

Ice Age flooding

However, at the end of the last Ice Age, flooding occured due to natural climate change. For example, the amount of water in the Mediterranean Sea increased greatly as the Earth warmed up and melted ice sheets. The water continued to rise and eventually broke a natural dam, sending a huge flood of water to fill what is now the Black Sea. If you'd been around to see it, it would have been terrifying!

Flash floods

Today, the most frightening floods happen very fast. They're called flash floods and are especially dangerous because they're always unexpected. The weather doesn't even need to be unusually wet. A flash flood can happen when a dying storm cloud suddenly releases all of its water in one torrential

LOG ON...
www.pbs.org/newshour/
infocus/floods

downpour. Then there's so much water it doesn't have time to soak into the ground and simply streams over the surface. If this water flows into a river valley, it can make the local river a raging torrent. With practically no warning, a wall of water, mud, huge boulders, and entire trees roars down into the valley, carrying

of the mountainside slid into the reservoir, travelling at close to 112 kmh (70 mph). This made a splash that sent an immense wave over the dam wall, and down the valley as a wall of water 69 m (230 ft) high. It swept through the

MOST OF THE WORLD'S FRESH WATER IS FROZEN INTO ICE

everything before it.

Flash floods can also happen if a big object, such as a tree, gets washed down a river and blocks it. Water collects behind this blockage and gradually builds up until the weight of it crushes and removes the blockage. Water then roars down into the valley below.

A terrifying flash flood in Italy in 1963 involved the Vaiont electricity dam. The water level in the reservoir behind the dam had risen to within about 12 m (40 ft) of the top of the dam wall, due to lots of rain. Then suddenly on 9 October, a whole section

village of Longarone, drowning everyone, and then flooding three more villages. The catastrophe lasted only 15 minutes, but it killed 2,600 people.

D evastating effects
Devastation like that is happening somewhere in the

A WOMAN IN BANGLADESH PREPARES A MEAL FOR HER FAMILY, DESPITE THE FLOODING INSIDE THEIR HOUSE.

59

this won't happen to you but for thousands of people it has.

Part of the problem is that people want to live near water and the fertile land it creates. Crops grow well in the soft flat soil, and there is water to use. But this, of course, is the land most likely to be flooded.

world right at this moment. There are families struggling to save themselves and their possessions. Thousands of other people die. Property is damaged and costs millions of pounds to rebuild. When the water does finally flow away, the mud that is left behind might be mixed with sewage, poisonous chemicals from factories, or oil. Imagine everything in your house becoming soaked and caked with muddy water? Hopefully

B loom not doom

Although their effects may seem terrible, floods can also be beneficial. The best rice is grown in fields that are flooded deliberately and the monsoon brings rain that makes the

THE THAMES BARRIER CONTROLS
THE AMOUNT OF WATER SURGING
UP THE THAMES IN LONDON, UK.

crops grow. The River Nile used to flood every year, bringing water and rich mud to fertilize the fields of Egypt. Farmers depended on it. Their crops fed people for thousands of years, as long as the river didn't become too full. This flooding doesn't happen now because the Nile is kept in check by the Aswan High the sea. If strong winds drive sea water towards the mouth of a river estuary, waves can take a surge of water up the river and flood the land to either side. This is called a storm surge. If a large surge were to flow up the River Thames it could flood parts of the London Underground train system and building basements.

THE ASWAN HIGH DAM PROVIDES HALF OF EGYPT'S ELECTRICITY

Dam, which was completed in 1970. This huge dam only allows measured amounts of water to flow along the river to the fields downstream.

Thames barrier
There are other ways of controlling a potential flood. One kind of flood that can be kept in check in London, UK, is one from

It would also drive sewage back through the sewers and out through manholes in the streets. Yuck! The Thames Barrier was built to prevent this happening, and the gates are quickly closed when a storm surge threatens London.

Humans can try to prevent some flooding disasters, but in many cases, the weather still has the upper hand.

DEADLY DROUGHT

Hot, dry, sunny weather can be great. But if the Sun continues to beat down, dry weather can become a drought with devasting effects. Crops fail, people die from hunger and thirst, and wild fires can destroy vegetation. If a drought continues, it may be impossible to bring the land back to life and eventually it becomes a desert, where only a few people and animals survive.

What is a drought?

The dictionary says that a drought is a prolonged period with little or no rain. How long it takes for a region to be considered in a drought condition depends on the amount of rain it usually gets. In the UK, 15 days without rain constitutes a drought and, in the United States, there's an official drought after 21 days in which the amount of rain is less than 30 per cent its normal amount. It takes an astounding two years without rain before a drought is declared in the Sahara desert.

IQUIQUE, IN CHILE, WENT FOR FOUR YEARS WITHOUT A DROP OF RAIN

In any inhabited area, drought is a potential killer. Thousands of people die as their crops fail and they are left with no food to eat or water to drink. Up to 250,000 people died in Ethiopia during a severe drought in 1973.

Parched ground

Droughts can occur anywhere, and the USA has had its share. The worst one happened in the 1930s in parts of Kansas, Colorado, Oklahoma, and Texas. The drought began in 1933 and before long, most of the plants had died, leaving the land bare. Without any vegetation to keep the soil together, it quickly turned to dust and the wind started to blow the soil away.

It blew so much away that at one time a single cloud of dust 5 km (3 miles) high covered a huge area from Texas to Canada, and from Ohio to Montana. Ducks and geese fell from the sky, choked to death by the dust. Dust settled on ships out in the Atlantic Ocean, nearly 500 km (300 miles) from shore. In the White House in Washington DC, as fast as they cleared the dust from the President's desk, more settled.

People called the dust storms "black blizzards" and the area that was affected by them came to be known as the Dust Bowl. This is because the soil was blown into massive dust dunes up to 10 m (30 ft) high. That terrible drought didn't end until the winter of 1940–41.

Forest fires

Lack of rain has other effects too. Where there's drought, there's also a risk of wildfires and they can be terrifying. Trees become drier and drier until they're like tinder, just waiting for a flash of lightning or a carelessly dropped match to set them on fire.

Once sparked to life, a wildfire can advance literally by leaps and bounds. Red and orange flames burst from the top of a tree, then another, and

ONLY THE HARDIEST PLANTS, LIKE THE CACTUS, CAN SURVIVE A DROUGHT.

another. Each blazing tree sends showers of sparks high into the sky to fall onto more trees, destroying the vegetation and everything living in it.

In 1983 a wildfire in Australia travelled as fast as a person can run. The heat was so intense that trees simply burst into flames spontaneously as the fire approached.

In another wildfire in 1993, flames reached the edge of Los Angeles, USA. Driven by winds up to 113 kmh (70 mph), the fire devoured vegetation that had dried out during a six-year drought.

DURING A DROUGHT, LAKES AND RIVERS MAY DRY UP, STRANDING WILDLIFE, SUCH AS THESE CATFISH IN AFRICA.

New life

Yet, when the deadly fire dies down, plant life often quickly begins again. Some plants rely on fires to remove their competitors. Certain pine trees will not drop their seeds until their cones have been scorched. Then the seeds can germinate in the nutrient-rich ashes and grow again.

Permanent drought

There are some places on Earth that experience a permanent drought. These places – deserts – cover almost a third of the surface of our planet. Arica, in the Atacama Desert in Chile, is one of the driest – it only gets about 0.7 mm (0.03 in) of rain each year. What's odd about Arica is that, while it's one of the driest places on Earth, it's also almost permanently cloudy. In fact, the air is so moist that wooden furniture rots and iron rusts! It just doesn't rain. That's because of the peculiar weather system there.

Air approaches the Atacama Desert from the west, across the Pacific Ocean. When it crosses a cold part of the ocean, the lowest level of air is chilled. This cold air is trapped below warmer, less dense air

A WILD FIRE RACES ACROSS THE DRY LAND OF KENYA, DESTROYING ALL IN ITS PATH.

above it, so it can't rise. Fog then forms instead of clouds, carrying only a tiny amount of water, leaving the Atacama extremely dry.

Sahara desert

The Sahara is the biggest desert in the world. This is one that looks like most people imagine a desert should look – miles of sand dunes shimmering in the intense heat. It stretches right across northern Africa, and receives less than 50 mm (2 in) of rain a year. For comparison, New Yorkers have to put up with about 1090 mm (43 in) of rain a year and Londoners with 556 mm (22 in).

WEIRD WORLD

DEATH VALLEY IN THE US GOT ITS NAME IN 1849 WHEN 30 PEOPLE USED THE VALLEY AS A SHORTCUT TO THE GOLDFIELDS. AIR TEMPERATURES OF 57°C (134°F) CAUSED 12 PEOPLE TO DIE FROM HEATSTROKE.

Dry and cold

People think of deserts as hot places, but they're not all hot. The coldest place in the world – Vostok, a Russian research station in Antarctica – is also a desert. Most of Antarctica is covered by a layer of ice and

snow 2 km (6,500 ft) thick, so how does it manage to be a desert? It's fairly simple. Very little snow falls, and what does fall, remains as snow because it is so cold. Near the South Pole there's no more than about 250 mm (10 in) of snow a year, which is equivalent to just 25 mm (1 in) of rainfall. This lack of rain officially makes Antarctica a desert.

Animal survival

Not many animals live in Antarctica, but in other deserts, small animals have developed novel ways to survive despite the lack of water. Gerbils and kangaroo rats are a good example. They eat seeds and other dry plant material, but never drink at all (although those kept as pets should be given water). They gather food at night when it's cool, and store it in their burrows where they rest during the day. The burrow is far enough below ground to stay nice and cool. The animal's moist breath makes the air inside the burrow damp and some of the moisture soaks into the dry food. When the animal eats its food, this moisture is recycled. Small desert animals manage to survive on this tiny amount.

Big animals, such as antelopes and gazelles, can't shelter in burrows. Instead, they feed at night when the leaves they eat absorb dew. This way, they get enough water to survive.

LOG ON...
http://www.ontheline.org.uk/explore/nature/deserts/deserts.htm

THE DESERT DUNES OF DEATH VALLEY, IN CALIFORNIA, USA

Helpful hump

One large animal –
the camel – has a
different trick. The
dromedary, the
one-humped
camel that lives
in hot African
and Arabian
deserts, has a
thick coat that
traps air next
to its skin.
This acts as a
cool insulation layer.

CAMELS ARE
ESPECIALLY ADAPTED
TO LIVE IN DESERTS.

than 480 km
(300 miles) in two
or three weeks,
without stopping
anywhere along the way
for a drink of water.

The hump also provides
insulation, and because it's
made from fat, it's a great
portable food store.

Camels don't sweat or urinate
much because they can't afford
to lose the water – and when
they are out and about, they
don't have to drink much
either. They can walk more

Beetle juice

You may think camels
have evolved smart
ways to live without
much water, but some beetles
are even smarter. Darkling
beetles live in the Namib
Desert of southwestern Africa.
It hardly ever rains there, but
fog often rolls in from the sea
during the night. On foggy
nights the beetles trot up to the
top of sand dunes and line up
in rows. Then they stretch their
long legs up and bob their
heads down, until their
hard, shiny, wing cases
are lifted almost
vertically. Droplets of
fog then gradually
collect on their
wing cases and
trickle down to
their mouths.

WEIRD WORLD
WHEN A CAMEL DOES DRINK, IT
DOESN'T KNOW WHEN TO
STOP! IT CAN GULP DOWN
103 LITRES (27 GALLONS) OF
WATER IN 10 MINUTES.
THAT'S THE EQUIVALENT OF
YOU DRINKING ABOUT
35 LITRES (9 GALLONS)
IN ONE GO.

This is the only water the Darkling beetles ever drink.

L iving in the desert

It is not just animals that live in deserts – people do too. In the vast, arid desert, small towns and villages have grown up around oases. Here, underground water rises to create rare patches of fertile land where crops, such as date palms, grapes, and figs can be grown.

Desert-dwelling people know how to keep cool. Traditional dress consists of several layers of flowing robes that cover people from head to toe. If you ever visit a hot desert these are the clothes that will keep you cool. The outer layer absorbs heat before it can reach your skin and, when you sweat, the warmth of your body makes your perspiration evaporate to keep you cool.

People and animals have adapted to living in the desert. But when a drought unexpectedly hits an area used to higher rainfall, it can be one of the worst kinds of extreme weather on Earth.

THE ROBES THESE MEN ARE WEARING HELP TO KEEP THEM COOL AS THEY WORK IN THE DESERT.

SPECIAL EFFECTS

Step aside Steven Spielberg! The Sun creates even more impressive special effects. We're all familiar with the beautiful rainbow, but don't forget the corona, the sundog, and the northern and southern lights – called auroras. These amazing effects happen when sunlight "plays" in the Earth's atmosphere, creating breathtaking light shows for us to admire – but you've got to be quick!

Rainbow of colour

The most common of these light shows is the rainbow. You'll see one when it's raining and sunny at the same time. The brightest rainbows, with the widest bows, generally appear early in the morning or late in the afternoon, when the Sun is low in the sky.

Light from the Sun bends and reflects off the inside surfaces of raindrops as it travels through them. Each of the seven colours that make up sunlight bends at a different angle. That's why all the colours appear in separate bands. Red always appears at the top of a rainbow, followed

A RAINBOW OVER KAUPO IN HAWAII

by orange, yellow, green, blue, indigo, and, last but not least, violet. A good way to remember these colours is to make up a sentence using the first letters of the colours (ROYGBIV) such as – Richard Of York Gave Battle In Vain.

Sometimes you might be lucky enough to see a fainter second rainbow, above the first one, with the colours in reverse order. This happens when light is reflected twice off the surface of each raindrop.

If you're ever flying in a plane when there's a rainbow, you'll see it as a whole circle, not just a bow.

Coronas, halos, and sundogs
Rings of coloured light can also surround the Sun – a ring that appears to sit around the edge of the Sun is called a corona.

WEIRD WORLD
THE SKY LOOKS BLUE BECAUSE WHEN BLUE LIGHT HITS AIR MOLECULES IT SCATTERS ALL OVER THE SKY, WHILE ALL THE OTHER COLOURS PASS STRAIGHT THROUGH THE AIR TO THE GROUND.

You can see this when there's a thin veil of cloud over the Sun. The corona is caused by tiny water droplets in the cloud bending the sunlight, just the way they do to make a rainbow. The Moon can also have a corona, and this shows up at night as a bright, white disc of light. It is white, rather than multi-coloured, because sunlight reflects off the Moon and through water droplets or ice crystals in thin cloud. This spreads the light out without breaking it into colours.

Another special effect is the halo. This is also a ring around the Sun and Moon, but it sits further away than the corona. It is formed in the same way as the sundog, or mock sun. A sundog appears as one or two bright spots of coloured light, often red with a white tail, near the Sun. They're made by falling ice crystals that bend the sunlight as they pass.

Curtains of light

Auroras are the most spectacular of all the Sun's special effects. These dazzling displays of coloured light can be seen at night near the Earth's North and South Poles. If you see them in the northern hemisphere, they're called "aurora borealis" or the northern lights, but if you're star gazing in the south they're called "aurora australis" or the southern lights. They look like huge curtains hanging high in the night sky, and rippling gently as if stirred by a breeze.

How auroras form

Auroras are caused by the solar wind – a stream of electrically charged particles propelled into space by storms on the Sun. The Earth's magnetic field traps some of the particles and pulls them down to the North and South Poles. When the particles crash into air molecules, their electrical energy is absorbed and released as coloured light. Oxygen molecules in the air make a greenish-white light, while nitrogen molecules make pink and blue light.

STORMS ON THE SUN SEND PARTICLES TOWARDS THE EARTH.

> **Warning**: never look directly at the Sun as it can permanently damage your eyes.

AN AURORA OVER ALASKA

POLLUTING THE AIR

The air that is moved around by the weather isn't always clean. Every day, harmful materials are released into the environment as a result of human activities. Many different types of pollution – arising from industry, transport, and energy use – enter the atmosphere and can affect our weather. We're beginning to understand and control the problem, but there is still more to be done.

Types of pollution

Pollution enters the environment in many forms and as a result of many activities. Air pollutants consist of gases and tiny particles of smoke, dust, and chemicals that are released from factory chimneys and vehicles. Their effects are worst in large cities and they are especially bad when a "lid" of warm air traps cooler air beneath it and the cooler air contains

INDUSTRIAL
CHIMNEYS IN
HAMPSHIRE, UK

pollutants. Smog is a problem in cities that are surrounded by hills, because that's where a layer of warm air is most likely to form. Car exhaust fumes react with each other in strong sunshine to produce a yellowish-brown haze that makes the air difficult to breathe. In 1989, Mexico City's smog was so bad that children were given a month off school.

Alternatives
Many governments are trying to persuade people to use their cars less to reduce pollution, but it is difficult. Environmental problems are not always given priority and public transport may not be reliable enough for people going to school or work.

Scientists are trying to tackle this issue by experimenting with fuel that creates less pollution than petrol. Some fuels have been developed, such as ethanol which is made from sugar cane, and burns cleanly. Hydrogen is the cleanest of all – when it burns it releases nothing but clean water. Alternative fuels can power vehicles, but ethanol is not widely used because it's expensive and hydrogen fuel is not yet available.

Ozone hole
Ozone, one of the helpful gases in our atmosphere, forms a layer in the stratosphere, about 25–50 km (15–30 miles) above

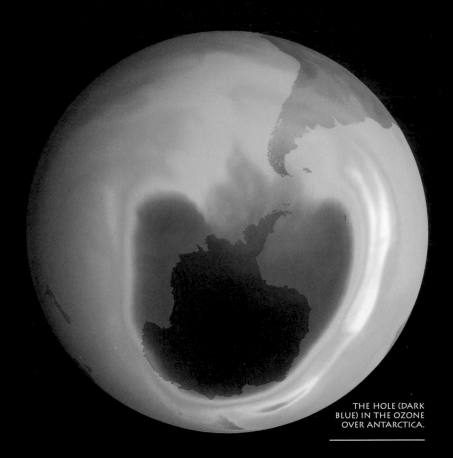

THE HOLE (DARK BLUE) IN THE OZONE OVER ANTARCTICA.

the Earth. This gas is vital because it absorbs much of the Sun's harmful ultraviolet radiation, stopping our skin from burning.

Some years ago, scientists discovered that the human-made gases – CFCs – used in refrigerators, air conditioners, aerosols, and some industrial processes – had damaged the ozone layer. In the 1980s a hole in the ozone layer was discovered over Antarctica, and there is now evidence that it has thinned over the Arctic as well. This means that more ultraviolet radiation is reaching us than ever before.

We've stopped making and

using CFCs, so eventually the hole will disappear. But this won't be until about 2050, and no one knows what damage could be caused by then.

Greenhouse gases

Another problem is the build-up of too many "greenhouse" gases in the atmosphere. In their natural state, greenhouse gases – carbon dioxide, methane and water vapour – act like glass in a greenhouse. They let the Sun's heat in, but they don't let all of it out again. This is called the greenhouse effect, and without it Earth would be largely covered in ice.

But humans have increased the amount of fossil fuels – such as coal, gas, and oil – that they use. When burned, these substances release carbon dioxide into the atmosphere, increasing the amount of greenhouse gases. Many scientists think this could make the world warmer. Droughts

could increase in some places and sea levels could rise, perhaps enough to flood some low-lying islands and coastal cities.

Global warming could also trigger extreme weather across the world. Not all scientists agree with this, but those who do are urging governments to reduce fossil-fuel burning.

Acid rain

Burning fossil fuels also causes acid rain. Car exhausts and burning coal emits gases

ACID RAIN HAS "EATEN AWAY" AT THE SURFACE OF THIS STATUE.

TINY PARTICLES
OF VOLCANIC ASH
DRIFT IN THE AIR. WHEN THE
SUN SETS, IT "CATCHES" THEM AND
PROJECTS THEM INTO BRILLIANT COLOURS.

that turn into acids. These strong acids can stick to the surface of buildings and statues in their dry state. They also dissolve in water to form acid rain that enters the ground or lakes, damaging plants, such as young pine trees, and fish.

Industries that burn coal and oil now have special filters that stop the emission of harmful gases. In many places, including North America and the European Union, cars are fitted with devices that drastically reduce the exhaust pollutants.

However, the number of cars is increasing, so although each causes less pollution, there are more cars. This slows recovery in areas damaged by acid rain.

Volcanic sunset

It's not only cars and factories that pollute the air. Some pollution is caused naturally – mainly by volcanoes. A big volcanic eruption throws water

vapour, gases, and ash high into the air. The smallest particles get thrown the highest, where they often remain, drifting around the world. If there's enough of them they can cause amazing sunsets. But they can also block enough sunlight to cool the Earth. When Mount Pinatubo, in the Philippines, erupted in 1991 it threw so much material into the stratosphere that in 1992 and 1993 the temperature at ground level was 0.4–0.7°C (0.7–1.25°F) less than average.

Positive thinking

Not all fuels are equally polluting. Natural gas, which is plentiful, is much cleaner than oil or coal. Soon it may be possible to use hydrogen as a fuel. Sunny and windy weather can also be harnessed to provide energy. One day solar cells on roofs may produce electricity from sunlight. Wind farms need space, but they can supply some power, especially to remote communities. Engineers are working on ways to obtain power from the movement of waves and tides.

These developments will help prevent pollution. But, what will reduce it most is changing the way we live. For example, the internet allows people to work from home, so they travel less and use less fuel. Hopefully one day the only way you'll learn about pollution will be from history books.

WIND POWER – AN ALTERNATIVE FUEL – PRODUCES POLLUTION-FREE ENERGY.

WEATHER WATCHERS

People have always needed to watch the weather. Farmers need to know if it will stay dry so they can harvest their crops, and fishing crews need to know whether they'll be a storm out at sea. Although there are some natural weather indicators, we generally rely on modern devices, such as satellites and weather stations, for this information.

IF THE FORECAST IS FINE, PINE CONES OPEN, BUT THEY CLOSE WHEN RAIN IS ON ITS WAY.

Natural forecasters

Using natural indicators, such as pine cones or seaweed, to forecast weather can be a bit hit and miss. For example, you need accurate measurements and you should also have an understanding of how the weather works.

SAILORS PREDICT STORMS FROM THE TYPE OF CLOUDS THEY SEE

seaweed goes soft and rubbery when the air is moist, and dry and brittle when the air is dry. This tells us what the air is like today, but not what it'll be like tomorrow. Some people in North America believe that if a groundhog sees its own shadow on 2nd February (Groundhog Day) in any year, then winter will last six more weeks. This may be true, but to make a reliable forecast

Satellite view

Weather covers the entire planet, so seeing everything at once isn't easy. It's only since 1960 that scientists have been able to see what's happening everywhere, all at the same time. That was the year the

A SATELLITE PICTURE OF EARTH, SHOWING A HURRICANE.

world's first weather satellite was launched.

Today, some satellites orbit the Earth at a height of about 850 km (528 miles), and pass over every part of the Earth's surface once every 24 hours.

Other satellites remain directly over the same point on the surface of the Earth. To do this, the satellite must be at a height of about 36,000 km (22,370 miles) above the Equator. At this height, a satellite takes precisely 24 hours to fly around the Earth, so it's always above the same place. These satellites can "see" almost half of the Earth at a time.

There are now many weather satellites in space belonging to different countries. But the information from them is shared. Together, they watch the whole of the Earth all the time. The pictures of cloud patterns that you see in television weather forecasts are based on images transmitted from these satellites.

LOG ON...
www.bbc.co.uk/weather/
weatherwise/diy

THIS AIRCRAFT
MONITORS AIR IN
THE UPPER ATMOSPHERE.

Satellites do more than just take pictures of clouds though. They measure the temperature and pressure at different heights, the temperature of the sea, and the extent of ice over the North and South Poles.

El Niño

Information from weather satellites has played a big part in helping scientists understand weather patterns like El Niño. This pattern occurs every five to seven years when the winds temporarily change direction over the Pacific, driving warm water east towards South America. The warm sea makes the air more humid, causing heavy rain and violent storms. At the same time, countries in the west Pacific, deprived of the warm ocean current, have very dry weather.

Weather stations

Weather satellites supply much of the information used to prepare weather forecasts, but not all of it. There are also weather stations down on Earth, located everywhere on land and sea – many of which are automatic.

A weather station measures air pressure, temperature, humidity, wind speed, and wind direction. At non-automatic stations, observers also record the cloud type and amount, visibility, amounts of rainfall or snowfall, and the present and recent weather.

There are also permanently

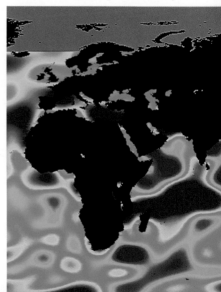

SATELLITE IMAGE SHOWS THE
WARM EL NIÑO CURRENT (RED)
WEST OF SOUTH AMERICA.

anchored weather ships equipped with meteorological instruments. These ships, as well as land stations, transmit instrument readings to a central office several times a day.

Aircraft are also used, but mainly for research. They have the scary job of flying through the middle of hurricanes and violent storms taking measurements of the conditions. Less dramatically, aircraft are also used to take samples of air for analysis.

A METEOROLOGIST ABOUT TO RELEASE A WEATHER BALLOON IN ANTARCTICA.

Balloons

Meteorologists also measure conditions high above the ground, using instruments that hang beneath balloons, called radiosondes. The balloons are filled with helium, and as they rise, their instruments radio measurements to the station. When they reach a certain height the balloons burst, and the instruments parachute to

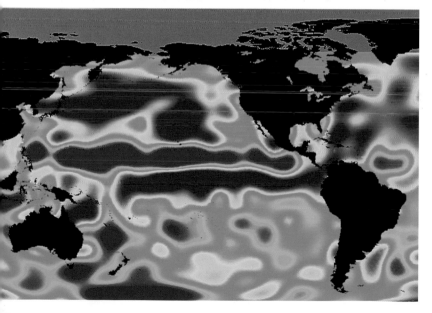

the ground. About 500 weather stations in the world release weather balloons at the same time – when it's midnight and noon at Greenwich, London.

Surface weather stations provide valuable information for weather forecasters, but they're not evenly distributed. There are many in North America and Europe, but not so many in Africa and Asia. Satellite measurements are therefore much more complete.

Weather forecasts

Once all the information reaches the meteorological office, scientists plot it onto maps, so they can see what the weather is like over a large area. The charts are kept up-to-date, so they show the direction weather systems are moving and their speed. This allows them to forecast when the weather will arrive over your house.

The forecast you see on television lasts just a few minutes, but preparing it was a big task. It involved satellites in space, weather balloons and stations on land and at sea, and the expertise of scientists and their computers. All this information gets put together, and helps you to make sense of the Earth's weather.

BLACK LINES JOIN PLACES WITH THE SAME AIR PRESSURE

COLD FRONT (BLUE)

WARM FRONT (RED)

WEATHER MAPS, LIKE THESE, ARE FORMED WHEN METEOROLOGICAL INFORMATION IS PUT TOGETHER BY SCIENTISTS.

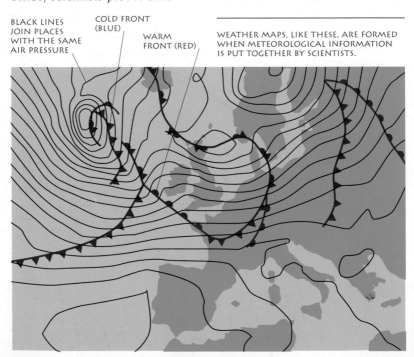

REFERENCE SECTION

Whether you've finished reading *Tornadoes*, or are turning to this section first, you'll find the information on the next eight pages really useful. Here are all the weather facts and figures, background details, weather classification charts, and unfamiliar words. You'll also find a list of website addresses – so, whether you want to surf the net or search out facts, these pages should turn you from an enthusiast into an expert.

WEATHER RECORDS

Coldest place
Vostock Station, Antarctica. On
21 July 1983 the temperature was
measured as −89.2°C (−128.6°F).

Hottest place
El Azizia, Libya. On 30 September
1922 the temperature reached
57.8°C (136°F).

Greatest extremes
Verkhoyansk, Siberia. The lowest
recorded temperature is −68°C
(−90°F), the highest 37°C (98°F).

Snowiest day
Bessans, France. An amazing
173 cm (68 in) of snow fell in
19 hours on 5–6 April 1969.

Biggest hailstone
The largest authenticated hailstone
fell on Coffeyville, Kansas, USA, on
3 September 1970 and measured
14.4 cm (5.7 in) wide and 0.77 kg
(1 lb 11 oz) in weight.

Rainiest place
Lloro, Colombia, is estimated to
have received an average 1,330 cm
(524 in) of rain a year for 29 years.

Driest place
Arica, in Chile's Atacama Desert,
had an average of less than 0.75 mm
(0.03 in) of rain a year over 59 years.

Longest drought
Tree-ring analysis shows that
southwestern USA suffered a 26-year
drought in the 13th century.

Strongest recorded wind gust
372 kmh (231 mph) at Mount
Washington, New Hampshire, USA,
on 12 April 1934. The winds in
tornadoes can be even faster.

Fiercest hurricane
Typhoon Tip, in the northwest
Pacific on 12 October 1979, had
sustained winds of 305 kmh
(190 mph).

Lowest air pressure
Pressure in the eye of Typhoon
Tip was 870 millibars.

Highest air pressure
A pressure of 1,083.8 millibars was
recorded at Agat, Siberia, Russia
on 31 December 1968.

Most severe tornado outbreak
In March 1925 a series of possibly
seven tornadoes (the Tri-state
Tornado) crossed Missouri, Illinois,
and Indiana, covering 703 km
(437 miles) and killing 689 people.

Worst American hurricane
At Galveston, Texas, USA, on
8 September 1900, a hurricane
killed 6,000 people, injured more
than 5,000, and destroyed half
the town's buildings.

Worst cyclone
In November 1970 a cyclone
moved from the Bay of Bengal
across Bangladesh, causing
floods that killed about half a
million people.

FUJITA TORNADO INTENSITY SCALE

Rating	Wind speed		Damage
	kmh	mph	
Weak			
F-0	64–116	40–72	Slight
F-1	117–180	73–112	Moderate
Strong			
F-2	182–253	113–157	Considerable
F-3	254–331	158–206	Severe
Violent			
F-4	333–418	207–260	Devastating
F-5	420–512	261–318	Incredible

AVALANCHE CLASSES

There are five classes of avalanche. Each class is ten times stronger than the one preceding it.

Class	Damage	Path width
1	Could knock someone over, but not bury them.	10 m (33 ft)
2	Could bury, injure, or kill someone.	100 m (330 ft)
3	Could bury and wreck a car, damage a truck, demolish a small building, break trees.	1,000 m (3,330 ft)
4	Could wreck a train carriage or big truck, demolish several buildings, or up to 4 ha (10 acres) of forest.	2,000 m (6,560 ft)
5	Largest known; could destroy a village or up to 40 ha (100 acres) of forest.	3,000 m (9,800 ft)

SAFFIR/SIMPSON HURRICANE SCALE

Category	Wind speed	Storm surge	Damage
1	119–153 kmh (74–95 mph)	1.2–1.5 m (4–5 ft)	Trees and shrubs lose leaves. Mobile homes slightly damaged.
2	154–177 kmh (96–110 mph)	1.8–2.4 m (6–8 ft)	Small trees blown down. Exposed mobile homes severe damaged. Chimneys blown from roofs.
3	179–209 kmh (111–130 mph)	2.7–3.6 m (9–12 ft)	Large trees blown down. Mobile homes wrecked. Small buildings damaged structurally.
4	211–249 kmh (131–155 mph)	3.9–5.4 m (13–18 ft)	Extensive damage to windows, roofs, and doors. Severe damage to lower parts of buildings near exposed coasts.
5	250+ kmh (155+ mph)	5.4+ m (18+ ft)	Catastrophic. All buildings severely damaged or destroyed. Major damage to lower parts of buildings less than 4.6 m (15 ft) above sea level to 0.5 km (0.3 mile) inland.

UV INDEX

UV Category	UVI value	Burn time (minutes)	Precautions
Minimal	0–2	30–60	Wear a hat.
Low	3–4	15–20	Wear a hat and use sunscreen SPF 15+.
Moderate	5–6	10–12	Wear a hat, use sunscreen SPF 15+, and keep in the shade.
High	7–9	7–8.5	Wear a hat, use sunscreen SPF 15+, keep in the shade, and try to keep indoors between 10 a.m. and 4 p.m.
Very high	10–15	4–6	Stay indoors as much as possible. When outdoors, wear a hat and use sunscreen SPF 15+.

ATLANTIC HURRICANE NAMES

2002
Arthur
Bertha
Cristobal
Danny
Edouard
Fay
Gustav
Hanna
Isidore
Josephine
Kyle
Lili
Marco
Nana
Omar
Paloma
Rene
Sally
Teddy
Vicky
Wilfred

2003
Ana
Bill
Claudette
Danny
Erika
Fabian
Grace
Henri
Isabel
Juan
Kate
Larry
Mindy
Nicholas
Odette
Peter
Rose
Sam
Teresa
Victor
Wanda

2004
Alex
Bonnie
Charley
Danielle
Earl
Frances
Gaston
Hermine
Ivan
Jeanne
Karl
Lisa
Matthew
Nicole
Otto
Paula
Richard
Shary
Tomas
Virginie
Walter

2005
Arlene
Bret
Cindy
Dennis
Emily
Franklin
Gert
Harvey
Irene
Jose
Katrina
Lee
Maria
Nate
Ophelia
Philippe
Rita
Stan
Tammy
Vince
Wilma

2006
Alberto
Beryl
Chris
Debby
Ernesto
Florence
Gordon
Helene
Isaac
Joyce
Keith
Leslie
Michael
Nadine
Oscar
Patty
Rafael
Sandy
Tony
Valerie
William

2007
Allison
Barry
Chantal
Dean
Erin
Felix
Gabrielle
Humberto
Iris
Jerry
Karen
Lorenzo
Michelle
Noel
Olga
Pablo
Rebekah
Sebastien
Tanya
Van
Wendy

BEAUFORT WIND SCALE

Force	Speed kmh (mph)	Name	Description
0	1.6 (1) or less	Calm	Air feels still. Smoke rises vertically.
1	1.6–4.8 (1–3)	Light air	Wind vanes and flags do not move, but rising smoke drifts.
2	6.4–11.2 (4–7)	Light breeze	Drifting smoke indicates the wind direction.
3	12.8–19.3 (8–12)	Gentle breeze	Leaves rustle, small twigs move, and flags made from lightweight material stir gently.
4	20.9–28.9 (13–18)	Moderate breeze	Loose leaves and pieces of paper blow about.
5	30.5–38.6 (19–24)	Fresh breeze	Small trees that are in full leaf sway in the wind.
6	40.2–49.8 (25–31)	Strong breeze	It becomes difficult to use an open umbrella.
7	51.4–61.1 (32–38)	Moderate gale	The wind exerts strong pressure on people walking into it.
8	62.7–74 (39–46)	Fresh gale	Small twigs torn from trees.
9	75.6–86.8 (47–54)	Strong gale	Chimneys are blown down. Slates and tiles are torn from roofs.
10	88.4–101.3 (55–63)	Whole gale	Trees are broken or uprooted.
11	102.9–120.6 (64–75)	Storm	Trees are uprooted and blown some distance. Cars are overturned.
12	more than 120.6 (75)	Hurricane	Devastation is widespread. Buildings are destroyed and many trees are uprooted.

WEATHER WEBSITES

www.fema.gov/kids
Information on tornadoes, hurricanes, floods, and thunderstorms.

www.wmo.ch/web-en/wmofact.html
The website of the World Meteorological Association.

www.nssl.noaa.gov/
The National Severe Storms Laboratory carries out investigations into all sorts of severe weather.

www.nws.mbay.net/history.html
A history of the US National Weather Service.

www.torro.org.uk/records.htm
British and European tornado and hailstorm extremes.

www.windpower.dk/tour/wres/coriolis.htm
Find out about the Coriolis effect.

www.nhc.noaa.gov/
Follow the expected course of the next hurricane with the help of the US National Hurricane Center's website.

www.miamisci.org/hurricane/index.html
Hurricane information from the Miami Museum of Science.

http://kids.earth.nasa.gov/archive/hurricane/index.html
NASA site for kids.

http://astro.uchicago.edu/cara/vtour/pole/
Take a virtual tour of the South Pole with the Centre for Astrophysical Research in Antarctica.

http://orpheus.ucsd.edu/speccoll/weather/27.htm/
Pictures of many different types of clouds from the International Cloud Atlas.
www.michaelallaby.com
Check out the author's own website.

http://kids.earth.nasa.gov/archive/air_pressure/index.html
Lots of experiments and information for kids.

TORNADOES GLOSSARY

Acid rain
Rain (and also snow, mist, or dry air) that is more acidic than ordinary rain due to pollution.

Climate
The weather conditions over a particular place, region, or the whole world, over a long period.

Climatology
The scientific study of climates.

Condensation
The change from gas to liquid.

Cumulonimbus
The scientific name for the dark, towering type of cloud that produces heavy showers, thunderstorms, hailstorms, and tornadoes.

Cyclone
An area of low air pressure. Also called a depression or low.

Desert
A region where the ground is dry because the average annual rainfall (or snowfall) is less than the amount of water that could evaporate from an open water surface in the course of a year.

Downdraught
The cold, descending air in a storm cloud.

Drought
A period when much less rain or snow falls than is usual for the place and time.

Dust devil
A spinning cloud of sand or dust that rises from the ground.

Flash flood
A flood that occurs suddenly, when a large amount of water flows downhill, sometimes because a river has overflowed.

Fog
Cloud that forms at ground or sea level and reduces visibility to less than 1 km (1,094 yd).

Hurricane
The name for a tropical cyclone that occurs in the North Atlantic Ocean, Caribbean Sea, or northeast Pacific Ocean.

Ice storm
A thick and rapid accumulation of ice on structures, such as trees, caused by rain freezing as it falls.

Inversion
A layer of warm air that traps cooler air beneath it.

Meteorologists
Scientists who study weather.

Meteorology
The scientific study of weather.

Mist
Minute water droplets that are suspended in the air, slightly reducing visibility.

Monsoon
The rainy season in South Asia, when the southwest monsoon wind blows, from about April to October. Monsoons also occur in many other parts of the tropics.

Mudslide
The rapid collapse of a hillside in a mass of sodden earth, trees and other plants, and rocks, that has been loosened by heavy rain melting snow, or earth tremors.

Smog
A form of air pollution that consists of either a mixture of fog and smoke, or a mixture of gases resulting from chemical reactions among pollutants.

Storm surge
An unusually high rise of the tide that occurs when storm winds drive water towards the coast.

Stratosphere
The layer of the atmosphere that lies above the tropopause, at about 8–16 km (5–10 miles), and extends to about 50 km (31 miles).

Tornado
A rapidly spinning vortex that descends from a storm cloud and touches the ground.

Tropical cyclone
A large, rotating storm, with torrential rain and winds of more than 120 kmh (75 mph), that occurs in the tropics. See also Hurricane and Typhoon.

Tropopause
The boundary between the troposphere and stratosphere, at about 16 km (10 miles) over the Equator, 11 km (7 miles) in middle latitudes, and 8 km (5 miles) at the North and South Pole.

Troposphere
The lowest layer of the atmosphere, extending from the surface to the tropopause.

Typhoon
The name given to a tropical cyclone in the Pacific Ocean.

Upcurrent or Updraught
Rising air inside a storm cloud. In a big storm cloud upcurrents can rise at 160 kmh (100 mph).

Vaporization
The change from liquid to gas.

Waterspout
A rapidly spinning vortex, similar to a tornado, that forms over water.

Weather
The atmospheric conditions of temperature, air pressure, wind, humidity, sunshine, and precipitation at a particular time and place.

Wind chill
The effect of the wind carrying away the layer of warm air next to the skin.

INDEX

CREDITS

Dorling Kindersley would like to thank:
Dawn Davies-Cook and Joanna Pocock for design assistance; Almudena Diaz and Nomazwe Modonko for DTP assistance; and Amanda Rayner for editorial assistance. Thanks also to Chris Bernstein for the index.

Additional photography by:
Peter Anderson, Brian Cosgrove, Andy Crawford, Alistair Duncan, Frank Greenaway, Dave King, Karl Shore, Clive Streeter, Eric Thomas, Jerry Young.

Picture Credits

The publishers would like to thank the following for their kind permission to reproduce their photographs:
c = centre; b = bottom;
l = left; r = right; t = top.

Agence France Presse: Steven R Schaefer 29c.
Associated Press AP: Dave Martin 43; Pavel Rahman Stringer 59bl.
Bruce Coleman Ltd: Pacific Stock 12bc, 70-1.
Corbis: James A Sugar 58tl; Steve Kaufman 6-7, 50.
Sylvia Cordaiy Photo Library Ltd: Nick Smyth 22tl.
Werner Forman Archive: Musee Royal de L'Afrique Centrale 17cr.
Fortean Picture Library: Hugh Gray 36tl.
Ronald Grant Archive: Universal Pictures & Warner Bros 32c.
Frank Greenaway: 34cr.
Robert Harding Picture Library: G Williams 38-39; Gene Moore/Phototake NYC 23bc; Michael Lichter/International Stock 8-9.
History Museum, Moscow: 52tl.
Hulton/Archive: 60tl.
Kristen Klaver: 33tr.
FLPA – Images of Nature: David Hoadley 31; Martin Withers 62-3.
Magnum: Steve McCurry 55.
National Maritime Museum: 72tc.
N.H.P.A.: A.N.T. 37.
NASA: 73bl.
Oxford Scientific Films: Konrad Wothe

5253; Mark Deeble & Victoria Stone 64bl; Martyn Chillmaid 18tc; R Toms 74-5; Steve Turner 65; Warren Faidley 6tl, 39bl.
Rex Features: 2, 26-27; Jean-Yves Desfoux/Sipa Press 4647.
Science Photo Library: Fed K Smith 85; Fred K Smith 1, 35; Gordon Garradd 78tc; Jack Finch 17; Jean-Loup Charmet 25; Joyce Photographics 83tr; Keith Kent 16-17; Macgrath/Folsom 19tr; NASA 83bc; NASA/SPL 76tc; NCAR 22br; Peter Menzel 24tl; Simon Fraser 77br.
Still Pictures: DRA 81; Jorgen Schytte 69br; Roberta Parkins 49; William Campbell 56tl.
Corbis Stock Market: 44bl.
getty images stone: 20-21; 278111001R 5; Ed Pritchard 44-45.
Telegraph Colour Library: Adrian Myers 48cr.
Woodfall Wild Images: David Woodfall 56-7, 79bc; Sean McKenzie 66-7.

Book Jacket Credits
Front cover
Science Photo Library: F.K. Smith
Back cover
National Maritime Museum
Robert Harding Picture Library: Gene Moore/Phototake NYC

All other images © Dorling Kindersley.
For further information see:

www.dkimages.com